To Shirin,

Hope this will remind you of your visit to Chichester and encourage you to return one day.

Hmie & David

12 October, 1955

Bookplate Ink

Ex Libris

Shirin Dastur Patel

CHICHESTER

CHICHESTER
A CONTEMPORARY VIEW

RICHARD PAILTHORPE

IAIN MCGOWAN

JOHN WILEY & SONS

Chichester • New York • Brisbane • Toronto • Singapore

Copyright © 1994 by John Wiley & Sons Ltd,
Baffins Lane, Chichester, West Sussex PO19 1UD, England
National Chichester (0243) 779777
International +44 243 779777

Introduction © Richard Pailthorpe 1994
Photography © Iain McGowan 1994 except where indicated

Other Wiley Editorial Offices

John Wiley & Sons, Inc., 605 Third Avenue,
New York, NY 10158-0012, USA

Jacaranda Wiley Ltd, 33 Park Road, Milton, Queensland 4064, Australia

John Wiley & Sons (Canada) Ltd, 22 Worcester Road, Rexdale, Ontario M9W 1LI, Canada

John Wiley & Sons (SEA) Pte Ltd, 37 Jalan Pemimpin #05-04, Block B Union Industrial Building,
Singapore 2057

British Library Cataloguing in Publication Data
A catalogue record for this book is available from the British Library
ISBN 0-471-95033-5

Designed, printed and bound in Great Britain by Butler & Tanner Ltd, Frome

ENDPAPERS
(*Front*) A portion of a map of Sussex described by John Norden and
'augmented' by John Speede dated 1610.
(*Back*) Survey of April 1812 by George Loader, Surveyor, as reproduced in *A History of the
Western Division of the County of Sussex* by James Dallaway Vol 1 dated 1815.

*To the memory of Bernard Price; a true Cicestrian whose writing
and broadcasting contributed so much to Chichester*

CONTENTS

FOREWORD
BY HIS GRACE THE 10ᵀᴴ DUKE OF RICHMOND

I have a collection of excellent books given to me by proud citizens of cities as far apart as Moscow, Los Angeles, Berlin and Bombay. In each case the book has enlarged my necessarily brief experience of its city, reminded me of my stay in later years and sometimes prompted or prepared my return visit. Open the cover and memory is revived and excited by the blend of written and visual images.

At long last the Chichester souvenir sees the light — souvenir in the French meaning of 'recollection, memory' — to be carried home by visitors from around the world who can later prove to themselves and to others the beauty and fascination of our enchanting Roman and Georgian city.

Today, Chichester, with its cathedral, theatre and other attractions has become an important centre of cultural life which draws people from all over the world.

I would like to congratulate Richard Pailthorpe on his imagination and industry in compiling the text and Iain McGowan in taking the large majority of the photographs.

To John Wiley and Sons Ltd, go my warmest gratitude and the thanks of the local community for their generous help towards the publishing of *Chichester - A Contemporary View.*

My family has been an integral part of Chichester and its life since the first Duke bought little Goodwood House in 1697. That was 12 years after his hapless half-brother, the Duke of Monmouth, was beheaded on Tower Hill for rebelling against his uncle, King James II. Monmouth had owned the Charlton Hunt which, subsequently revived, had brought the first Duke of Richmond to Goodwood.

The second Duke repaired the Market Cross at his own expense and made a hefty contribution to the erection of the City Council House in North Street.

The third Duke was High Steward and Mayor of the City as well as building most of Goodwood House and starting Goodwood Races.

It was in the 1920s at the Market Cross that my grandmother, Hilda, the eighth Duchess, driving an early motor car, was confronted by a traffic policeman who held up his hand to stop her. Affronted, she leaned out of the window and cried, 'Get out of my way, you silly man', and he did!

Well, times have changed. I do not hunt and I obey traffic policemen, I make modest contributions to new projects and I sit on committees and I write 'forewords' to books, hoping to maintain the family's contribution to this precious jewel of a city that is Chichester.

INTRODUCTION

Chichester is the county town of West Sussex, and one of England's smallest cathedral cities. It owes much of its charm and character to a long and enticing past. The photographs which have been selected for this book reflect the fascinating history of the city and its surrounding area, as well as showing the lively, modern place Chichester is today. They also capture the beauty of the contrasting local landscapes, ranging from the Downs to the coastal plain and Chichester Harbour.

The origins of Chichester can be traced back two thousand years to the period before the Roman conquest in AD 43. The hill known as the Trundle, which still dominates the Downland skyline to the north of the city, was first occupied during the Neolithic period (c.5000–4000 BC). The Iron Age hillfort dates from the 4th century BC and was probably abandoned in about 100 BC. Archaeological evidence indicates that Iron Age settlements were located near to the site of the modern city.

The Romans established Chichester as a military base. The local tribe, called the Atrebates, were friendly to the invading Romans and it is possible that their King, Tiberius Claudius Cogidubnus, lived in the magnificent palace at Fishbourne. The Romans called Chichester, *Noviomagus Reginorum*, meaning 'new market of the proud people'. It became the capital of the local kingdom and the region must have enjoyed a great deal of prosperity. The town had a number of important buildings, including a forum, public baths and a temple dedicated to Neptune and Minerva. The present cruciform town plan and the city walls originated during the Roman period. An amphitheatre occupied a site just outside the East Gate and the remains of a number of villas have been discovered in the surrounding countryside. With the death of Cogidubnus, *Noviomagus Reginorum* became part of the province of Brittania.

The Romans left Britain at the beginning of the fifth century, and within fifty years parts of Sussex had been colonised by the invading Saxons, whose leader was named Aella. Little is known about Chichester during this period although two important episodes have been recorded. First, it was one of Aella's three sons, called Cissa, who made the former

The livestock or 'beast' market took place every other Wednesday and was held in the main streets until 1870. Old photographs and engravings show the streets crowded with all sorts of animals. In North Street the wattle pens of calves, sheep and pigs stretched from the Cross to Northgate. At the beginning of the 19th century the historian, Dallaway, recorded that the market was the second largest in the country after Smithfield. It is probable that this was due to the proximity of Chichester to Portsmouth, and the need to supply the Navy during the Napoleonic wars.

By 1870 the dirt and congestion created by the market led to it being moved to a new site near the East Gate.

Roman town his base and renamed it Cissa's ceaster meaning 'Cissa's camp'; the name Chichester is thought to derive from this.

Then, in 681, St. Wilfrid, the exiled Bishop of York, landed near Selsey. Selsey was, at this time, the main cultural centre of the region. St.

Despite being one and a half miles from the city, the wharf at Dell Quay acted for centuries as Chichester's nearest accessible port.

Wilfrid's preachings converted the local Saxons to Christianity. A monastery and a cathedral were built, although we do not know exactly where they stood.

Chichester would have acted as a refuge for the inhabitants of the area, who, it is recorded, defeated a plundering army of Danes during the late 9th century. After 1066, the Norman policy of centralisation was instrumental in bringing about the transfer of the Bishop's seat from Selsey to Chichester in 1075. This decision probably did more than anything else to change the course of Chichester's history.

Sussex was divided by the Normans into administrative districts known as 'Rapes'. The Rapes of Chichester and Arundel were granted to one of William the Conqueror's most loyal supporters, Roger de Montgomery.

Work started on the present Cathedral during the latter part of the 11th century, and building was to continue throughout much of the Middle Ages. The Cathedral has had many eminent and outstanding Bishops, but the most famous was St. Richard of Wych, who was Bishop between 1245 and 1253. His popularity meant that pilgrims flocked to Chichester to visit his shrine until its destruction during the Reformation.

During the Middle Ages Chichester grew in importance, not only as a cultural centre but also despite its distance from the sea as an important port and market town for the region. A Merchants Guild charter was granted in 1135 and by the 13th century Chichester was made a Staple, giving it a monopoly of the local wool trade. However it was not until 1501 that Bishop Story built the Market Cross. This was his gift to the poorer tradesmen, as it created a market place where they could sell their goods free from local taxes.

While the south-west quadrant of the city housed the Cathedral and

(Left) *The Market Cross at the turn of the century.*

(Below) *A view of East Street at the turn of the century. On the left, a horse chestnut tree can be seen next to the Corn Exchange.*

(Overleaf) *Southgate and the railway station during Goodwood Race Week at the turn of the century. The railway reached Chichester in 1846.*

associated ecclesiastical buildings, the city's trading and business activities, including the beast market, were carried out in the north-east quadrant. A motte and bailey castle had been built by the Normans in what is now Priory Park. This was destroyed during the early 13th century and shortly afterwards the Grey Friars built a priory on the site. The priory was dissolved in 1538, leaving only the chancel, which still stands today; it served as a Guildhall and now it is part of the District Museum.

At the beginning of the English Civil War in 1642 the local population was divided in its allegiance. The city declared its support for Parliament, but by mid-December, Sir Edward Ford, the County Sheriff had taken control in the name of King Charles I. However, on 21 December, Sir

William Waller, with some 6,000 Parliamentarian troops, began to lay siege to the city. On 29 December, it surrendered to Waller and remained Parliamentarian for the rest of the war.

The main damage which occurred during the siege was to the Eastern suburb of St. Pancras. After the surrender, the interior of the Cathedral was ransacked and Royalist sympathisers, notably the clergy, suffered reprisals.

It is interesting to note that some of the local citizens played a prominent part in the politics of this turbulent time. William Juxon, an ex-pupil of the Prebendal School, was chaplain to Charles I at his execution in 1649. In 1660 at the Restoration of Charles II, Juxon became Archbishop of Canterbury. In stark contrast, Chichester's

Member of Parliament, William Cawley, was one of the regicides who signed Charles I's death warrant. He had also been a pupil of the Prebendal School. A local landowner, Colonel George Gunter of Racton and a Chichester merchant called Francis Mansel assisted the future King Charles II in his escape from Oliver Cromwell after the battle of Worcester in 1651.

Today, Chichester is renowned for its Georgian architecture. However, as we learn from James Spershott, a local resident during the 18th century, this was not the case during the early 1700s. He writes, in his intriguing account of life in Georgian Chichester, that 'the city had a very mean appearance at this time'. Furthermore, 'the buildings were in general very low, very old, and their fronts framed with timber which laid bare to the weather, and had a step down from the street to the ground floor, and many of them over the first floor projected further into the street. The shops in general had shutters to let up and down, and no other enclosure, but were quite open in the daytime, and the penthouse so low that a man could hang up the upper shutter with his hands. There were very few houses even in the main streets that had solid brick fronts except such as appeared to have been built within a few years back.'

A considerable transformation took place during the 18th and early 19th centuries. Many of the fine buildings that were erected or improved are still standing for us to enjoy today. Some splendid examples of Georgian domestic and public architecture can be found not only in the main streets but also in St. Martin's Square and the Pallants. The Pallants are to be found in the south-east quadrant and reflect in miniature the city's main street plan. A cross, demolished in 1713 stood in the centre.

Goodwood Racecourse during the late 19th century. Racing had been started at Goodwood by the third Duke of Richmond in 1801. The grandstand seen here was built in 1830 by the fifth Duke and could accommodate 3,000 people. It was pulled down in 1903 and replaced by a new grandstand. The course was open at this time, and the road from Chichester to Singleton was little more than a chalky track.

The Archbishop of Canterbury held this part of the city as a palatinate until 1552; the name Pallant derives from this.

The 18th century also saw the development of the great country estates in the area. The third Duke of Richmond during the second half of the century increased the size of the Goodwood Estate from 1,000 to nearly 18,000 acres. Of more significance to local residents was the introduction of racing in 1801. Goodwood Race Week, traditionally held during the last week of July, was an important week of the year for many people.

A view of West Street, taken during Goodwood Race Week in 1912.

Before the days of motor transport thousands of race goers would flock to the area and find board and lodgings in hotels, inns and private homes.

Even after a century of prosperity, Victorian Chichester was described by some residents of the period as being 'dull' and 'sleepy'. It was, however, a very important market centre for the farmers of the region, who brought business to the local shops, inns, banks, auctioneers and solicitors.

One major drama that all Victorian Ciscestrians would have been aware of was the collapse of the Cathedral spire in 1861. This took five years to rebuild.

It is our good fortune that little major development took place during

The Cathedral spire collapsed at 1.30 p.m. on Thursday 21 February 1861. The collapse was the result of structural weakness, which had been under repair. It happened after a severe storm and amazingly none of the workmen was killed. Sir Gilbert Scott was commissioned to rebuild the spire to its original design. The fixing of the weathervane on the newly reconstructed spire took place on 28 June 1866. The spire rises to a height of 277 feet (84.4 metres) and is the only one in the country visible from the sea.

the late 19th and early 20th centuries. County Hall was not built until just before the Second World War, in the then comparatively undeveloped north-west quadrant of the city. German air raids were to cause some damage to Chichester during the war and it is lucky that the city did not suffer more in view of its proximity to RAF Tangmere and other satellite airfields.

Other projects of major cultural interest have included the discovery of the Fishbourne Roman Palace, the creation of the Weald and Downland Open Air Museum at Singleton, and the restoration of Pallant House as an historic house and art gallery. The Mechanical Music and Doll Collection and Tangmere Aviation Museum have been founded in recent years. The stately homes of Stansted and Goodwood are both open to the

(Left) *Regrettably, Sharp Garland's shop in Eastgate Square had to be demolished in 1964. It claimed to be the oldest grocery shop in Britain, having been in continuous use since 1665.*
(Above) *The busy Avenue de Chartres inner ring road now runs where cattle once grazed in the Westgate fields.*

Like many towns and cities, Chichester has experienced its greatest changes during the post-war years, as it has strived to cope with the ever-increasing problems of motor transport and a growing population. Sadly, most of the family-owned shops and businesses have gradually disappeared and cows no longer graze up to the city walls in the Westgate fields. At the same time, many exciting developments have happened. Chichester has become one of the most important cultural centres in Southern England with its internationally famous Festival Theatre and the annual arts festival known as the Chichester Festivities.

public and host a wide range of events and activities. At West Dean, the Edward James Foundation is an important centre for teaching the arts and crafts. Chichester Harbour is designated an 'area of outstanding natural beauty', and offers probably the best sailing for small boats in the country. A trip on the harbour water bus or a walk along the shoreline will reveal many species of birds and plants.

Nearly 50 years ago Dr Thomas Sharp wrote that Chichester 'is a living and lively as well as a lovely city', and those words apply equally today.

A major Roman public building possibly stood on the site of the Cathedral. Part of this 2nd century mosaic was discovered in 1966 and is on display in the Cathedral.

THE ORIGINS

The city of Chichester, with its Cathedral spire, is the focal point of this panoramic view from St. Roche's hill. The Iron Age fort at the top of the hill is known as the Trundle; it was abandoned in about 100 BC in favour of a new site beneath or close to modern Chichester.

Under the eye of the Trundle, the Chichester District Archaeological Unit excavates an Iron Age settlement on a site scheduled to become a reservoir, near East Lavant.

A school party on the Trundle survey the view from the ramparts of the former Iron Age hillfort. The Trundle became a permanently occupied enclosure, defended by a series of concentric ditches, during the Neolithic period. During the Middle Ages, a chapel dedicated to St. Roche was built on the hilltop, and a windmill, which burnt down in 1773, was built on the site of the chapel. A gibbet also once stood on the hill.

In the past the Trundle played an important part in communications. A signal beacon was sited on top of the hill during times when invasion threatened. Today, only two radio masts out of the eight that were erected during the Second World War remain.

The Romans connected Chichester to London by building Stane Street in about AD 70. It is just over 57 miles in length and some of the best preserved sections, which are near Eartham, are owned by the National Trust.

(*Left*) The city walls are Roman in origin and date back to the 3rd century. They run for one and a half miles forming an irregular polygon around the city. They were originally built of earth with a facing of flint and mortar, with two ditches beyond them. The walls we see today are medieval, based on the Roman foundations. The last occasion they gave protection to the city inhabitants was during the English Civil War in 1642. The city gates were demolished during the late 18th century and a promenade walk was formed around sections of the walls. A walls walk can still be enjoyed today.

During the 4th century southern England was under the threat of attack from marauding Saxons. The Romans strengthened the city's defences by building bastions, such as this one in Market Avenue.

A view of the Cathedral from the Bishop's Palace Garden. The Bishop's Palace and the gardens are approached from Canon Lane through a gatehouse dating from 1327. The gardens are open daily to the public and are managed by Chichester District Council. A local historian, Alexander Hay, described them (in about 1725) as having been 'laid out in a plan of great beauty and elegance'.

THE CITY

A view of the Cathedral from the south east. The Norman Cathedral was built on the site of a Saxon church, St. Peter's. Building began during the Episcopate of Bishop Ralph Luffa (1091–1123), and the east end was dedicated in 1108. The Cathedral was severely damaged by fire twice during the 12th century. The second fire occurred in 1187 soon after the church had been consecrated. Reconsecration took place in 1199 and throughout the next two centuries major building work continued.

The 12th century nave showing
the striking John Piper tapestry
behind the high altar, designed
in 1966.

St. Richard is regarded as the patron saint of Sussex. His appointment as Bishop of Chichester in 1245 took place in contentious circumstances, following a dispute with King Henry III, who refused to recognise his appointment. As a result his income was withheld and he had to rely on charity for his living for two years, before the King relented. He died in 1253 at Dover and was canonised in 1262. His remains were laid to rest in the shrine in Chichester Cathedral in 1276.

St. Richard's Day is celebrated on 3 April, and it is recorded that the pilgrims who crowded into the Cathedral on this day had to be restrained from physically fighting for precedence. The pilgrims, through their offerings, contributed great sums to the Cathedral. The traders and innkeepers of the city must also have benefited greatly from their custom.

The shrine of St. Richard was destroyed during the Reformation in 1538 and it is recorded that there were enough jewels, precious stones, rings and silver gilt images taken from it to fill seven chests. The tapestry behind the altar, on the site of the shrine in the retro-quire, was designed by Ursula Benker-Shirner and woven at West Dean and in Bavaria. This is also the burial place of one of Chichester's best known Bishops, George Bell (1929–1958).

A view of St. Richard's Walk from Canon Lane, looking towards the cloisters.

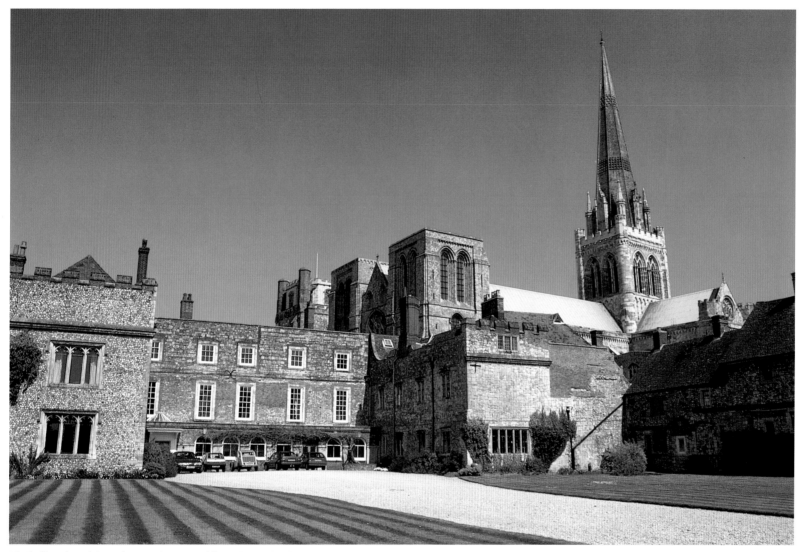

The half-H plan of the Bishop's Palace viewed from the south. The palace was probably rebuilt after the fire of 1187, and over the centuries additions and alterations have been made. The old kitchen, which is used for performances during the Chichester Festivities, contains an excellent example of an early medieval 'hammer beam' roof. The private chapel contains one of the country's most important early Gothic wall paintings, known as the Chichester Roundel, depicting the Madonna and Child.

The cloisters, which date from the 15th century, enclose a former burial ground, known as 'Paradise'.

The 'Wayfarer' window in the
cloisters, made in 1909, depicts
St. Nicholas and St. Richard.

The rounded arch of a Norman or Romanesque doorway.

The font in the baptistery was designed by John Skelton and is made of Cornish polyphant stone.

After the great fire of 1187, the rebuilding of the Cathedral was carried out using a Jurassic stone quarried from Caen in Normandy. Throughout its history the Cathedral has required repair and restoration, particularly in modern times. The Friends of the Cathedral have raised considerable funds towards this work and in 1965 the Cathedral Works Organisation was founded to carry out maintenance and restoration work. The organisation also undertakes work on other historic buildings requiring the expertise of skilled stone masons.

The statue of William Huskisson. He was a former Member of Parliament for Chichester, who has the misfortune to be remembered as the first person to die in a railway accident. In 1830, as President of the Board of Trade, he was attending the opening of the Manchester to Liverpool railway when he was accidentally run over by George Stephenson's 'Rocket' locomotive.

This memorial by John Flaxman on the south wall of the bapistery is to William Collins (1721–1759), the son of a Chichester hatter, who was also Mayor. Collins was educated at the Prebendal School, Winchester and Oxford. Regarded as Chichester's best known poet, he led a rather tragic life and is buried in St. Andrew-in-the-Oxmarket Church, which is now the Chichester Centre of Arts.

This stained glass window was designed by Marc Chagall in 1978 and made by Charles of Marq. It illustrates Psalm 150, 'O praise God in his holiness... Let everything that breathes praise the Lord!'.

Cathedral environs.

Chichester has the distinction of having the only surviving detached Cathedral bell tower or campanile in the country. It dates from the first half of the 15th century and has also been known as Raymond's Tower. The bells are housed in the octagonal lantern at the top of the tower.

The Market Cross at night.

Built in 1501 at the city's focal point, where the four main streets meet, the Market Cross was the gift of Bishop Story (1478–1503). It was a place where poorer tradesmen could sell their goods free from local taxes. His deed of gift reads: 'To the Sucoure and Comfort of the Poore Peple there... a Crosse sett and founded yn the midde of the said cite... no housez shoppez nor stallez to be bilded... nigh adjoynyng... to the lett or dist'baunce of the poore peple to sell their chafer there...'. The main produce market was moved in 1808 from the Cross to the newly erected Butter Market.

Over the centuries the cross has been added to as well as receiving substantial repair and restoration. Like the Cathedral, it is constructed of Caen stone. It managed to survive circumnavigation by all kinds of motor transport, until relief came through the pedestrianisation of the main streets.

South American musicians perform in front of the Market Cross.

The Market Cross viewed from West Street.

This view of South Street shows the old theatre on the right, which was rebuilt in 1791. The building remained a theatre until 1850, after which it has endured a number of uses, ranging from a brew house, to a small shopping mall.

Traffic driving through the main streets would have made this view of North Street impossible twenty years ago. Pedestrianisation of the city centre, particularly of North and East Streets, took place during the late 1970s and early 1980s.

In 1591 Queen Elizabeth I visited Chichester and it is alleged that she stayed in a property belonging to John Lumley, Earl of Scarborough. This building, in East Street, is now the Old Punch House and Lindy Lou luggage shop. The audience chamber in which the Queen met the mayor and citizens of the city is now the shop, and still contains the magnificent Tudor ceiling decorated by Italian craftsmen.

The Old Punch House was famous for the making and sale of a liqueur known as 'Chichester Milk Punch', which could evidently be drunk at any time of the day. It was a favourite drink of Queen Victoria who, in 1840, appointed the then proprietor, John Hudson, 'to the place of manufacturer of Milk Punch to her Majesty' by Royal Warrant.

During the 18th and early 19th centuries Chichester prospered and many fine buildings were erected, giving rise to it being regarded as a 'Georgian City'.

These three elegant buildings with bay windows are to be found in North and South Streets.

When Pallant house was built in 1712 by Henry 'Lisbon' Peckham, a young wine merchant, it cost £3,000 of his wife's £10,000 fortune, an awesome sum when a good townhouse could be built for about £500. Pallant House was reopened as an historic house and art gallery in 1982. The faithfully restored rooms and reconstructed Georgian garden each reflect a particular period of the house's history. They also provide a lively backdrop for the fine antique furniture, pictures, porcelain and textiles that visitors can discover as they move from room to room, and from the age of Hogarth to the last years of Queen Victoria's reign. The 20th century is represented by the gallery's holdings of modern British art from two private collections. Artists represented include Henry Moore, Graham Sutherland, Ben Nicholson, Paul Nash and Barbara Hepworth.

City rooftops viewed from Pallant House.

Pallant House has also been known as Dodo House. The ostriches, the Peckham family crest, sit on top of the gate piers and have been mistakenly referred to as dodos.

The expense to which Henry Peckham went in building Pallant House is reflected in the high standard of craftsmanship, both inside and out. Note the finely gauged brickwork over the tall narrow windows, each with a carved emblem in the keystone. The overhead ornamental wrought ironwork between the gate piers leading to the Corinthian doorcase, carries the monogram H.P. which can be read both ways, by those entering or leaving the house.

The city's timber-framed buildings were either rebuilt or refronted around the turn of the 18th century. Both Dillons bookshop and the White Horse Inn (*right*) are examples of medieval buildings with an overhanging upper storey, known as a 'jetty'. The gateway to Canon Lane (*above*), known as Canon Gate, was probably built during the 16th century and was restored extensively in 1894. It now houses the administrative offices of the Chichester Festivities. A 'Court of Pie Powder' was once held in the upper room to collect the bishop's tolls and hear disputes arising from Sloe Fair.

(*Below left*) These houses in the Vicar's Close date from the 15th century and originally formed part of the College of Vicars Choral. Today, some are the official residences of the Cathedral staff while others are occupied by people closely associated with the ongoing life of the Cathedral. The frontages of the houses on the opposite, western side, were reversed in 1825. Now they are shops facing onto South Street. A wall which still stands, was built, to separate them from the Close. The remainder of the former Close was demolished in 1831.

A terrace of 19th century cottages in Orchard Street.

A view from the city wall, looking onto the backs of 19th century houses in Orchard Street.

(*Far left*) A terrace of Georgian cottages in East Pallant.

The former Corn Exchange is an unlikely location for a McDonald's restaurant. It was built by George Draper, a local architect, between 1832 and 1833. The main entrance is through a six-column Greek Doric portico. Chichester, being the centre of an important grain growing area, was one of the first towns to build a Corn Exchange. Inside, local farmers met dealers and merchants who hired the desks and stands on which sample bags of wheat, oats and barley were set out for inspection.

As a public building the Exchange was, by the end of the 19th century, becoming used for other purposes, notably for theatrical and social functions. It housed the city's last cinema, the Granada, before conversion to a McDonald's.

The Oliver Whitby School, now the A & N department store. The motto Vis et Sapientia ('Strength and Wisdom') can still be found over the main entrance door.

The building dates from 1904 and replaced an earlier school house on the site. The school had been founded by Oliver Whitby in 1702 'for 12 boys, with a view of qualifying them for especially the sea service'. The school was a Blue Coat school and closed in 1950 when it amalgamated with Christ's Hospital School, near Horsham.

The Butter Market was built for the City Corporation in 1807 and opened in January 1808. It was designed by the well-known Regency architect John Nash. Entered through an imposing portico, it provided covered space for market stall holders away from the dirty and congested streets.

Stall holders contributed towards the cost of the building by paying tolls on the sale of their produce, which included such items as 'butter, cheese, pickled pork, fowls, cockles and mussels, crabs, dead hogs and turnips'.

(*Below*) The City Council and its committees meet in the Council Chamber. The chandelier dates from the 18th century and the panels around the chamber contain the names of the city's Mayors since 1531. Chichester's first recorded Mayor was Emery de Rouen in 1239.

1607	PETER PALMER	1656	WILLIAM STAN
1608	EDWARD LAWRANCE	1657	JOHN WOOD
1609	JOHN EXTON	1658	FRANCIS HOBS
1610	THOMAS BRIGGHAM	1659	RICHARD MITC
1611	JOHN RANSOM	1660	WILLIAM BUR
1612	RICHARD KEARE	1661	ANTHONY WIL
1613	JOHN CAWLEY	1662	JOHN GREENF
1614	GEORGE ANDREW		Died March 5
1615	BENJAMIN HOOKE		MARK MILL
1616	WILLIAM STRUDWICK		Served out
1617	THOMAS NORTON	1663	NICHOLAS EX
1618	THOMAS FARRINGTON	1664	THOMAS BUR
1619	THOMAS COLLINS	1665	EDWARD EXT
1620	HENRY SHELLY	1666	THOMAS VAI
1621	JOHN SHALAT	1667	RICHARD YO

The Council House in North Street was designed by Roger Morris and built in 1731. It was paid for by public subscription. An inscribed Roman stone referring to King Cogidubnus, discovered nearby in 1723, suggests that the Council House stands close to the site of a Roman temple dedicated to Neptune and Minerva. The stone is now displayed under the portico.

The Assembly Room, which was added in 1783, was designed by James Wyatt. The ante-room contains showcases displaying civic insignia, including the mace. Also on show are silver and plate, and Royal charters granted to the city.

The Mayor of the City (1993–4), Mrs. Anne Scicluna, accompanied by the Parade Commander, Major Huw Edwards, inspects the Princess of Wales' Royal Regiment, to mark the Honorary Freedom of the City granted to this newly formed Regiment in 1993. The Freedom, which is the highest honour a city can give was first conferred on The Royal Sussex Regiment in 1951. Mrs. Scicluna has twice been Mayor, a position also held by her father.

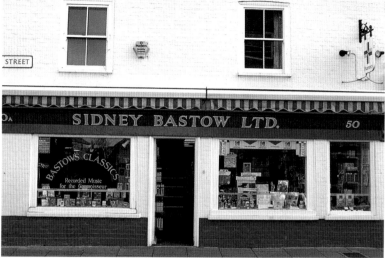

Today, only a small number of traditional shops and businesses remain in the city.

At the turn of the century, the writer W.H.Hudson, had some disparaging remarks to make about the large number of public houses in the city; there were 70 at the time. He commented that men could be found, 'pipe in mouth and tankard in hand' drinking at 8 a.m. and at closing time, 'a goodly crowd of citizens are seen stumbling forth'.

Great changes have occurred since the sad decision to close the livestock market was taken in 1990. Today, a trading market takes place every Wednesday and Saturday, and for the remainder of the time the site is devoted to car parking. However, some traditions, such as the bicycle sale remain.

Soon after the Norman Conquest, Roger de Montgomery built a motte and bailey castle on the present site of Priory Park. The castle was destroyed in 1217 but part of the motte still survives. From 1269 to 1538 a priory of the Grey Friars existed on the site of the castle.

After the priory's dissolution, the chancel, seen behind the bowling green, was converted into a Guildhall, and it was also used as a courthouse. In 1804, William Blake, writer of the hymn 'Jerusalem', was tried here for sedition. The Guildhall now houses part of the District Museum.

Priory Park became the property of the Duke of Richmond in 1824, and in 1918 the 7th Duke presented it to the city as a war memorial. Bowls have been played in Chichester since at least the 17th century.

Cricket was first played in Priory Park in 1851. James Lillywhite, who
captained the first England side to play against Australia in 1877, played
for Priory Park. W.G. Grace as well as two visiting Australian sides have
played in the park. Sussex played first class county cricket here until 1950.

The origins of Sloe Fair, held annually on 20 October, date back to the early 12th century when King Henry I made a grant to the Bishops of Chichester to hold an eight day long fair. Sloe Fair was held in a large field, near the North Gate, called 'Sloe-field', after a tree which grew there. The tolls and profits from the fair were paid to the bishop. The fairground is now the Northgate car park.

The City Fair first took place in 1987 to mark the centenary of the local newspaper, The *Chichester Observer*. Organised by the *Observer* and the Chichester Lions Club, stallholders donate their 'pitch fee' to charity. The 1993 fair had a 'Roaring Twenties' theme.

The 13th century church, All Saints in the Pallant, is now the head-quarters of the local branch of the Red Cross. William Hayley, the poet, was baptised in the church in 1745.

The redundant medieval church of St. Andrew-in-the-Oxmarket lies just off the north side of East Street, and is now the Chichester Centre of Arts. The poet William Collins is buried here, as is John Cawley, three times mayor of the city and father of William Cawley, the regicide and founder of the Cawley Almshouses.

The Saxon church on whose site the Cathedral was built, was dedicated to St. Peter. A subdeanery church continued to be located within the Cathedral until the mid 19th century when a new, separate church, St. Peter the Great, was built in West Street. Today it is an antique and craft arcade.

Musicians from the Royal Academy of Music perform at St. John's Church during the Chichester Festivities. The church was built in 1813 to a design by James Elmes, who lived at Oving. It is one of the country's finest examples of a chapel built in the 'low church' tradition. With its galleries it seated 622 people. Its great glory is the three-in-line pulpit made of American black birch.

Built because of the lack of accommodation for the city church-goers of that time, it was soon so popular that, with the doors wide open, sermons were being preached to a congregation that extended out into the street. This overflow caused the church authorities to have another church built and a further one restored.

St. John's then lost half its membership and half of its income. Subsequent financial troubles, from which it never recovered, caused its closure in 1976. It then passed into the care of the Redundant Churches Fund, who have put in hand the much needed restoration of the building.

The Chichester Festivities began in 1975 as a special one-off event to mark the 900th anniversary of the foundation of Chichester Cathedral. The instant popularity of the Festivities ensured an encore in 1976, and soon it became a founder member of the British Arts Festivals Association. The festival now ranks as one of Britain's twenty leading arts festivals.

(*Right*) '*Sculpture in Paradise*' a temporary exhibition of contemporary, sculpture held during the 1993 Festivities. Administered through the Hat Hill Sculpture Foundation, the pieces will one day form part of '*Sculpture at Goodwood*', at a location near Goodwood.

Activities centre on the Cathedral with other events happening at Goodwood. A spectacular fireworks concert takes place at the Racecourse, and chamber concerts are performed in the ballroom of Goodwood House. In addition venues in the city and within the Chichester area play host to numerous fringe events.

A juggler busking on the Cathedral Green during the Chichester Festivities.

The Festival Theatre has maintained an international reputation since its first season in 1962, which was directed by Laurence Olivier. Described as the 'Impossible Theatre' it was founded by Leslie Evershed Martin, who conceived the idea whilst watching a television programme on a January night in 1959. The programme was about the building of a Shakespeare theatre in the small Canadian town of Stratford, and inspired Leslie Evershed Martin to establish a theatre in Chichester.

A site was chosen in Oaklands Park and the £105,000 needed to build the theatre, was raised by private fundraising, public subscription and commercial sponsorship. The theatre's running and maintenance costs are still funded from these same sources. The architects Powell and Moya broke away from tradition by designing a hexagonal stage with an auditorium containing nearly 1400 seats, with each one being no further than sixty feet away from the stage.

The Festival Theatre viewed from Oaklands Park against the backdrop of the Cathedral.

Over the last thirty years a galaxy of theatrical stars including Olivier, Alec Guiness, John Gielgud, Derek Jacobi, Kenneth Branagh, Judi Dench and Donald Sinden have appeared at the theatre. The adjoining Minerva Theatre was opened in 1989; as well as having its own season of plays and films, it is also a base for educational and youth theatre.

The Festival Theatre is one of Britain's leading theatrical producers, and many of its productions transfer to the West End.

Harry Secombe performing in
Pickwick during 1993.

Theatregoers mingle before an
evening performance.

St. Mary's Hospital is hidden behind a row of cottages in St. Martin's Square. The building dates from the end of the 13th century. Its external appearance has changed little, but over the centuries a number of internal alterations have been made in the interests of residents. The timber-framed aisled hall of the infirmary and chapel is one of the earliest and finest examples of 'a crown-post collar purlin roof' in south east England. The medieval hospital had few internal walls, and the beds would have been arranged along the side walls in the aisles. It would have provided temporary accommodation for travellers and the sick. They were cared for by a small mixed community of brothers and sisters under the custos (or guardian) who was a priest.

At the Reformation responsibility for the hospital passed to the Dean and Chapter. Ever since, they have been trustees of the hospital and are responsible for its maintenance and administration.

The hospital today is in charge of a matron. The custos, an Anglican priest, is responsible for worship in the chapel and the pastoral care of the residents. Accommodation for four married couples and eight single persons is provided in the main building and in adjacent cottages.

At the heart of the life of St. Mary's today, as for the past 700 years, is the daily worship in the chapel, which is a condition of residence. The public can view the hospital by appointment with the matron.

The Royal West Sussex Hospital was opened as the Chichester Infirmary in 1826. The foundation stone had been laid by the Duke of Richmond a year earlier.

Medical history was made here, when the stethoscope was first used in this country by John Forbes, Honorary Physician to the infirmary.

King George V renamed the infirmary, the Royal West Sussex Hospital, in 1913 in memory of his father, King Edward VII. The wisteria growing on the front is claimed to be the oldest in the country. It was planted when the infirmary was built and came from China.

The Hospital and Chapel of St. Bartholomew, also known as Cawley's Almshouses were built during 1625-26 by William Cawley, to house, in the buildings on either side of the chapel, 'twelve decayed tradesmen' from Chichester.

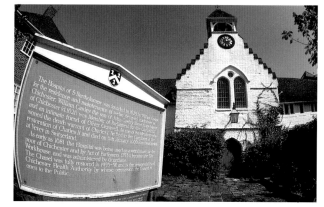

(*Right and centre*) This small cottage near the corner of Spitalfield Lane and St. Pancras adjoining the River Lavant, is all that remains of St. James' Hospital for lepers; built during the early 12th century it was destroyed by fire in 1781.

William's father John, was three times the City Mayor and a major brewer. William born in 1602, carried on the family business and at the age of 25 became the Member of Parliament for Chichester. He later sat for Midhurst and again for Chichester. During his time in Parliament he joined Cromwell's party, and during the Civil War was an important figure in the area. He was appointed one of the judges at the trial of Charles I, and along with others, became a regicide by signing the King's death warrant in 1649. With the Restoration he had to flee the country. He died in 1666 in Switzerland and it is believed that his son secretly had the body carried home and buried in this chapel.

During the 18th century the hospital was taken over by the City Council as a poor house, and was subsequently enlarged. In the 1920s it became one of a number of workhouses administered by the West Sussex County Council. It operated until 1946 when it was taken over by the local health authority and the workhouse closed.

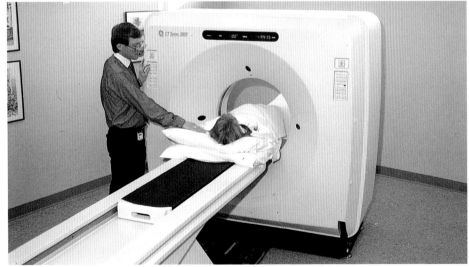

In November 1990 a scanning suite was built at St. Richard's Hospital thanks to the generosity, supreme effort and hard work of the people of Chichester and its surrounding area. The benefit of C.T. scanning over conventional x-rays is in its ability to clearly define the soft tissues of the body, thus assisting doctors in a fast and accurate medical diagnosis with minimal discomfort to the patient.

A replica Marlborough bucket boot in black leather, manufactured during the period 1700–1712, hangs over Clarks shoe shop in East Street. The original boot is on display in the Clark Shoe Museum at Street in Somerset. The Chichester shop is one of only four in the country with such a sign.

A wishbone sign hangs outside the factory of C.Shippam Ltd. Shippam's of Chichester have long been famous for their pastes. The business has been based in Chichester for over 200 years; in the 1850s, they employed two assistants and served only the local area. Major production of Shippam's pastes started in 1892 when Charles Shippam set up a factory behind his butcher's shop in East Street. By 1909, 46 men were employed. In 1912 a larger factory was built alongside the East Walls. Since then the factory has been greatly extended. In 1924 the main entrance in East Street was built and in 1953 the large packing building was added.

The Westgate Centre has the head of a Roman centurion as its emblem. It was opened in 1987 and provides the city with a wide range of indoor leisure facilities, including swimming pools and a sports hall.

(*far right*) This leaping dolphin can be seen in St. Martin's Street. Carved in wood, it is the work of John Skelton, the sculptor and letterer, who was Eric Gill's nephew and last apprentice. Another example of Skelton's work, *Symbol of Discovery*, is located outside the District Museum.

Today, Shippam's main production still takes place on this site within the city walls. Shippam's products are taken from Chichester for international distribution. Shippam's remains an important local company employing over 400 people.

Despite its controversial design, the Avenue de Chartres car park, which opened in 1990, has won a Civic Trust and other architectural awards.

At the beginning of the 17th century a thriving needlemaking industry was centred on the eastern suburb of St. Pancras. Much of this area was destroyed during the Civil War and the industry never fully recovered, although it survived in a small way until well into the 18th century. Its decline was equally attributable to the increased and cheaper competition from other parts of the country. Today this busy ring road and a terrace of flats serve as a reminder of this once flourishing cottage industry.

This view from the Cathedral shows the north-west quadrant of the city, now dominated by the West Sussex County Council administrative buildings. The circular County Library was designed by the County Architect, F.R. Steele and took five years of planning before opening in 1967. This part of the city was comparatively undeveloped until well into this century. A house, known as the Grange, and described as a 'gothic fantasy'. was demolished in 1962 to make way for the expansion of the County Hall.

The new Tourist Information Centre in South Street, was opened by the actress Susan Hampshire in July 1993. It is managed by Chichester District Council and deals with over 100,000 enquiries each year.

Considered by the architectural historian, Alec Clifton-Taylor, to have the most imposing house front in Chichester, Edes House, was built by John Edes, a maltster and his wife Hannah, who completed the building after his death in 1696. Their initials can be found in the tympanum over the front door and on some of the rainwater downpipes.

In 1916, West Sussex County Council acquired the property having decided to make Chichester the administrative centre for the county. It became the County Hall, but various Council departments had to be located in other buildings in the city. By the 1930s the need to centralise everything was recognised. A new County Hall was designed by Cecil Stillman, County Architect. He was assisted with

the building programme by Stanley Roth, who was later to become a senior member of the County Council. It was built in the former orchard to the rear of the house, and opened in 1936. The house then became the County Library headquarters.

In 1967 the house was occupied by the County Record Office, which subsequently moved to new premises in 1989. The house has since been extensively restored, and is now used by the County Council for meetings as well as for artistic and cultural events.

Chichester Nursery School—
young Cicestrians of the future.

Sports day for the pupils of the Prebendal School. The school is the oldest in Sussex and its origins probably go back to the time when the Cathedral was moved from Selsey to Chichester, during the late 11th century. It was at this time a 'song school', responsible for housing and teaching choristers. The school was refounded in 1497 by Bishop Story. The school's name is derived from the Prebend of Highleigh, a canonry, which Bishop Story made into an endowment to fund the school. The school is now a preparatory school for 200 boys and girls.

The College of Arts, Science and Technology was opened in 1964 and currently has 10,000 students of which 2,300 are fulltime, studying 'a wide range of academic, commercial, scientific, technical, recreational and adult education courses'.

Pupils from Chichester High School for Boys ponder over a game of chess. The school was formed in 1971 when the High School for Boys, a grammar school founded in 1928, and the Lancastrian Secondary School, which had been founded in 1810, amalgamated as a comprehensive school.

The New Park Centre is housed in the former Central Boys School, which was rebuilt in 1887 and could accommodate 390 boys. Today, the community association members using the centre include the Chichester Players and the New Park Film Centre. During three weeks of the year plays are performed by the Players, an amateur drama group established in 1933.

Bishop Otter College was founded in 1850, in memory of Bishop Otter, Bishop of Chichester from 1836 until 1840. In 1839 he had established a small college in Little London for the training of male teachers. The college amalgamated with Bognor Regis College in 1977 to form the West Sussex Institute of Higher Education. The institute has also been designated as a college of the University of Southampton.

This converted granary at Northgate, dates from the late 18th century. The conversion has retained, on the brick facade, the name of its former occupants, the Chichester corn merchants, Bartholomews.

Chichester District Museum tells the story of how local people lived and worked, in country and town, in the most western part of Sussex. The Chichester district is a varied area stretching from the Downs in the north to the coast in the south.

Highlights of the museum include displays of Roman objects, such as jewellery, tools and a newly-displayed mosaic, all excavated in the local area. A later part of the local story is told in the display 'Chichester the Market Town' which traces the growth and subsequent decline of the local markets through recollections of people who worked in them. The museum's displays also illustrate recent changes in local trades, shops and transport.

The museum is based in 29 Little London. The building was formerly a corn store. In the early 1900s it was bought by Sadler and Company, agricultural merchants. At this time trades linked with local agriculture were still vital to the prosperity of the Chichester area. By the 1960s this had changed and several buildings in Little London fell into disuse. The architect Stanley Roth was instrumental in preserving the street as it is today. In 1963, 29 Little London was converted to form a home for Chichester's museum.

Several original features remain, including a large crane on the side of the building which was once used for hoisting sacks. A story which claims that the street was named Little London by Queen Elizabeth I on her visit to the city must be regarded as false, because there is reference to the name a century earlier.

As well as its permanent displays, the museum offers special loan services for schools and a lively programme of changing exhibitions and events. Here, curatorial staff are seen preparing for a new exhibition.

Clive and Enid Jones set up their unusual museum in the redundant Victorian church of All Saints at Portfield in 1983. Over the years the family had amassed an amazing collection of Victoriana — especially mechanical musical instruments, natural history items, and dolls. It was often suggested to them that they should display these treasures, and so they decided to set up the Mechanical Music and Doll Collection. Clive's aim is to display every item as it was when first made. He and his son, Lester, have restored them to their original condition and in full working order.

A plaque on 11 Eastgate Street records that John Keats began to write 'The Eve of St. Agnes' there.

'St Agnes' Eve — Ah, bitter chill it was!
The owl for all his feathers, was a-cold;
The hare limp'd trembling through the frozen grass,
And silent was the flock in woolly fold:'

This stone stands in Broyle Road, adjacent to the boundary fence of the Barracks. Near this spot, six smugglers were hanged in January 1749, for the atrocious murder of a customs house officer, William Galley, and a shoemaker, Daniel Chater. The smugglers had originally met in Charlton forest over a year earlier to plot a raid on the customs house at Poole. After the raid Galley and Chater, who was a key witness, had been on their way to give evidence on oath to a magistrate near Stansted. They stopped at the White Hart Inn at Rowlands Castle, where the smugglers were informed of their presence. Desperate to escape arrest, they murdered the two men.

The murders created public outrage and seven smugglers were eventually arrested and condemned to death. One of them died a few hours after sentence was passed, but the remaining six were hanged on Broyle heath, where the stone was erected to serve as a public warning.

The site of a Roman amphitheatre can be found just off the Hornet. It was possibly built around AD 70, and would have been used as a place of public assembly and entertainment. The latter would have included animal baiting and circus performances with acrobats and tumblers.

Suffolk House Hotel in East Row was built in about 1736 and was once the town house of the Dukes of Richmond.

It is probable that the Dolphin and Anchor Hotel stands on part of the site of the Roman forum. The Dolphin and the Anchor were originally two inns competing against each other for business, particularly during the heyday of stage coaching at the turn of the 19th century. The Dolphin was also a venue for cock fighting at this time. The two inns amalgamated in 1910.

The Ship Hotel was built by Admiral Sir George Murray as his private house, towards the end of the 18th century. It has interesting military connections. Murray, who was born in Chichester in 1759, had a distinguished naval career, and served under both Sir John Jervis and Horatio Nelson. He led the Fleet at Nelson's victory at the Battle of Copenhagen in 1801. He died in 1819, and the following year 200 dozen bottles of wine were auctioned from the house cellars.

The house became the Ship Hotel shortly before the Second World War. In April 1944 General Eisenhower stayed at the hotel and it was here that he met with General Montgomery, Admiral Cunningham and Air Chief Marshal Sir Arthur Tedder, to plan part of the D-Day operations.

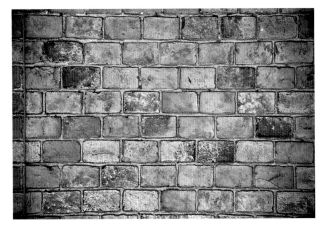

Different examples of brick colouring can be found throughout the city. By the 18th century, it was common to lay bricks in Flemish bond, alternating a brick laid sideways, known as a 'stretcher', with a brick laid end on, known as a 'header'. Often, the 'header' brick would be glazed or coloured grey or blue, thus creating an attractive chequer pattern. Coloured bricks were used more extensively to give an overall grey appearance to the facade of a house, in contrast to the more commonly used red brick.

Many of the houses to be found in the north-east quadrant, particularly in St. Martin's Square, Lion Street and Little London, demonstrate the rebuilding that took place in the city during the late 17th and throughout the 18th centuries. This early 17th century house was refaced in brick with stone dressings towards the end of that century by its owner Sir John Farrington.

A window in Washington Street. This street, along with Parchment Street and Cavendish Street, forms a part of Old Somerstown. The character of this late Georgian suburb, just outside Northgate, was lost when the three other streets which made up the community of old Somerstown were demolished in the 1960s, to make way for the present Somerstown development.

Door furniture. Foot scrapers are a reminder of the days in previous centuries when the city streets were not as clean as they are today.

  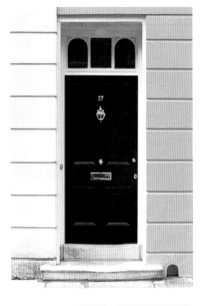 

A wealth of Georgian doorcases and fanlights can be discovered throughout the city.

The 1993 Beer Barrel Race at Chichester canal basin. The winner received 18 gallons of beer plus £100. The ladies won four bottles of gin plus £50!

During the Middle Ages Chichester and its harbour were considered to be one of the country's major ports. This is perhaps hard to imagine, as the city itself is not on the sea. The cargoes had to be brought up the harbour to Dell Quay, where they were laboriously transferred into wagons to complete their journey by road. A proposal to connect the city to Dell Quay by canal was first made at the end of the 16th century; but it was not until 1822 that the idea became a reality, with the construction of the Portsmouth to Arundel Canal. The four and a half mile long section of the Chichester Canal was built by John Rennie at a cost of £170,000. It could take vessels of up to 150 tons and the main cargo carried was coal. The canal was never a commercial success and the last cargo was carried to the canal basin in 1906.

The canal is now being developed as a recreational and leisure amenity. The Chichester Canal Society aims to restore through navigation between Chichester and the harbour.

West Wittering beach looking towards East Head (the most open part of Chichester Harbour).

CHICHESTER HARBOUR AND THE SEA

This stretch of the canal at Hunston is popular with walkers and anglers. It was from here that Turner painted his famous view of the Cathedral in 1830.

Mist over the harbour, near Dell
Quay.

Houseboats and waterlilies are
now resident on the last stretch
of the canal at the Chichester
Yacht Basin.

Managed by Chichester Harbour Conservancy, Chichester Harbour extends to some 11 square miles of inter-tidal waters and 17 miles of navigable channels. Between the 17th and 19th centuries it was a busy commercial harbour, exporting wheat and malt. Through the Chichester Canal the port was linked to the then extensive waterway transport system of this country. Today the harbour has virtually no commercial traffic, but provides ideal water space for recreational yachting, and a base for a small but active fleet of professional fishermen as well as for amateur angling. Over 9,000 vessels are on record at the harbour office paying an annual harbour dues fee. With over 5,000 moorings the harbour makes a substantial contribution to water-based recreation in the Solent and the south.

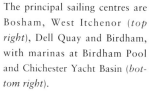

The principal sailing centres are Bosham, West Itchenor (*top right*), Dell Quay and Birdham, with marinas at Birdham Pool and Chichester Yacht Basin (*bottom right*).

Chichester Harbour Water Tours (*bottom left*), based at West Itchenor, was started in April 1983 by Peter Adams. Before then there were no facilities for the public to tour Chichester Harbour by boat. The company began with one boat, *Wingate I*; demand for the tours was such that *Wingate II* had to be added to carry additional customers who wished to see the harbour and its wildlife at closer quarters.

Bosham from across the harbour at high tide.

(*Right*) Sunset over Bosham.

Sunset over the harbour at Bosham.

Unsuspecting motorists often return to find their cars have been caught by an incoming tide. Although the story has been dismissed by modern historians, legend has it that it was at Bosham that King Canute (1016–1035) sat in his chair and attempted to command the tide to turn back.

Wall painting at Bracklesham.

The astronomer Patrick Moore — Selsey's most famous resident — with one of his many telescopes situated in his garden observatory. Selsey is well known for its clear skies and atmosphere.

East Beach at Selsey, looking towards the lifeboat station built in 1960. It replaced an earlier one, built in 1927, whose distance from the shore had increased in the intervening period by nearly half a mile as a result of coastal erosion. As a fishing village, Selsey has always been famous for its shellfish, particularly crabs and lobsters. This century, it has become well known for its caravan parks and as a holiday resort.

The *City of London*, Selsey's Tyne class lifeboat is launched from the boathouse. Selsey's first lifeboat station was established in 1861 by the Royal National Lifeboat Institution 'for the protection of the crews of vessels which got stranded on the Ower's Banks and other shoals in the neighbourhood of Selsey Bill'.

Selsey Bill is the most southerly point on the Sussex coast. Selsey was, in effect, an island until the early 19th century, and this exposed peninsula has been gradually eroding away for centuries.

Pagham Harbour is one of the few undeveloped areas of the coast in West Sussex. The open landscape still retains a sense of wilderness, and is very popular with ornithologists. The harbour was reclaimed for agriculture in the late 19th century but was flooded again by a storm in the early 20th century. The harbour and the surrounding pasture are of international importance for wintering wildfowl and waders. The area has been managed as a Local Nature Reserve by the County Council since 1964. Extending to some 1,500 acres the reserve encompasses a mosaic of habitats including large areas of salt-marsh and mudflats intermingled with shingle beaches, reedbeds and wet grasslands.

(*Right*) A view of Sidlesham, looking across Pagham Harbour towards the site of the tidal mill. The mill became redundant in 1876, when this once busy harbour was reclaimed for agriculture. However, at Christmas 1910, torrential rain and flooding caused the sea to break through the defences, and the reclaimed land reverted to look as it was before 1876. The mill was demolished in 1913.

The unspoilt sandy beach, by the entrance to Chichester Harbour at West Wittering, has been popular since the 1920s with bathers, and more recently windsurfers. It regularly receives Clean Beach and Water Quality awards.

The Schneider Trophy, an international trophy open to seaplanes, was contested off West Wittering when it was won outright by Great Britain in 1931. The contest was watched by Sir Henry Royce, the famous engineer who designed the winning Merlin Aero engine. He lived in the village, and had his drawing office there. Nearby is the prominent Tudor tower of Cakeham Manor, a former residence of the Bishops of Chichester.

In 1954 the beach and surrounding land were put up for sale by the Church Commissioners. In order to rescue it from holiday camp and caravan park development, local residents formed the West Wittering Protection Society, now West Wittering Estate plc, who still own and manage it.

Windsurfers at West Wittering.

Near East Ashling.

THE COUNTRYSIDE

The 13th century church of St. Michael, situated in the remote Downland hamlet of Up Marden. It was described by Pevsner as having 'one of the loveliest interiors in England'.

Cardinal Manning, who was once curate to the rector at nearby Graffham, wrote 'The Hills... Upwaltham Church...The Downs seem to me only less beautiful than Heaven'.

William Cobbett travelled through Upwaltham on one of his Rural Rides in 1823. The hamlet lies at the head of the upper Lavant Valley. The 12th century church, of St. Mary the Virgin, described by Pevsner as 'untouched and lovable', still retains its original plan, with a rounded chancel or apse.

St. Andrew's Church at West Stoke dates from the 11th century, and the nave contains a portion of a recently restored 12th century mural. Members of the de Bathe family are buried here. The family lived nearby at Woodend; Sir Hugo de Bathe was a husband of Lily Langtry, the famous Edwardian actress, and friend of King Edward VII.

The tiny 12th century Downland church of St. Mary at North Marden, is one of four Sussex churches still retaining its original simple plan with a rounded chancel or apse.

St. Wilfrid's chapel is all that remains of Selsey's former parish church which was removed from Church Norton to its present-day site in Selsey in 1866, leaving only the chancel. It dates from the 13th century, and the original church may have been built on or near the site of St. Wilfrid's cathedral church. There were 25 Bishops of Selsey between 681 and 1075, before the Bishopric was transferred to Chichester.

The 13th century church of St. Peter at East Marden with the thatched village well-head in the foreground. The date of the well-head is uncertain, but it would appear to have been built by the mid 19th century.

The 13th Century church of St. Margaret at Eartham is interesting for the memorials it contains to some of the former occupants of the adjoining Eartham House. William Hayley, the poet, lived there between 1774 and 1800, and there is a monument in the church to his son, Thomas, carved by John Flaxman. Famous visitors to Eartham House at this time included the historian, Edward Gibbon, the poet, William Cowper and the artist, Romney.

William Huskisson bought the house from Hayley and a tablet in the church records his death in a railway accident in 1830. Another monument to him can be found in Chichester Cathedral.

The church at Bosham may have been built on the site of a small monastery; said to have existed prior to the coming of St. Wilfrid. Bosham was an important Saxon settlement, and the church tower dates from this time. It is probable that the powerful nobleman, Godwin, Earl of Essex, had a residence at Bosham.

The Bayeux Tapestry shows Godwin's son, Harold, praying at Bosham Church in 1064 prior to his ill-fated journey across the Channel. He was shipwrecked off the coast of Normandy and fell into the hands of Duke William. The Normans claimed that before returning to England, Harold took an oath renouncing his claim to the English throne. Harold subsequently became King on the death of Edward the Confessor in 1066 and this led to the Norman invasion, which changed the course of English history. Bosham has, over the centuries, been well known for ship building and as a fishing port, but today it is best known as a recreational sailing centre.

The church of St. Mary the Virgin at Apuldram is of 12th century origin but was almost entirely rebuilt in the 13th century. Apuldram is a shrunken medieval village, at the edge of Chichester Harbour, near Dell Quay. The church and the small manor house, known as Rymans, which was built in the early 15th century, survive from this period. Nearby is Apuldram Roses, a specialist rose nursery open to the public.

A variety of building materials can be discovered in the local villages: brick and timber framing at West Ashling (*top left*) and Sidlesham (*bottom left*); flint at East Dean (*centre left*) and Singleton (*right*); and 'Mixon' stone at Selsey (*below*). The latter is a limestone and was once quarried from the Mixon Reef, off Selsey Bill.

Cottage window at Oving.

The village pond in East Dean is the natural collecting point for the spring water that feeds 'Chichester's river' — the Lavant. This small seasonal stream takes its name from the word 'levant' or 'lavant', meaning 'landspring'. Traditionally, the springs break out in mid-February, or earlier during a wet winter. It flows some nine miles southwards, around Chichester, and eventually into the harbour near Apuldram.

The River Lavant flows through East Lavant, one of the villages named after the river. The 19th century historian, James Dallaway, records that the village 'is pleasantly situated on small eminences, falling in every direction to the rivulet, Lavant, which is particularly broad and shallow'.

Behind the river a pair of 'Duchess cottages' can be seen. During the second half of the 19th century the sixth Duke of Richmond, anxious to improve the welfare of his tenants, built 49 distinctive pairs of flint cottages on the Goodwood Estate. They contained three bedrooms, a kitchen, living room and pantry; in addition each pair had a separate outhouse containing woodsheds, privies and a communal wash house with an oven and copper. The origin of the term 'Duchess cottage' is uncertain although it probably relates to the interest the sixth Duchess of Richmond expressed in their design.

Mr and Mrs Upton at Slindon have an international reputation for their pumpkins, which provide an unusual and colourful attraction to the village each autumn.

A glasshouse at the Manor Nursery, Runcton, containing 87,000 geraniums, claimed to be the biggest crop in Sussex. A grand total of 135,000 were grown at the nursery in 1993.

Fetes of all descriptions take place each weekend throughout the summer months. At West Dean (*right*), the 1993 fete raised funds for the village school, whilst at Up Marden (*below*), proceeds went towards the restoration of the church roof.

Don Wilkinson, the village farrier, working at his forge in Funtington.

A flinty field on the Downs.

(*Right*) Barn near Earnley built with rounded beach flints or cobbles.

A winter landscape near Goodwood.

The Downs near Upwaltham.

West Dean House from the park.

(*Left*) A College Diploma student of metalwork restoration.

(*Right*) Students on a short course in the courtyard at West Dean College.

West Dean House is one of the finest flint mansions in the country and stands on ground which has been occupied since medieval times. In 1891 the house and its estate were bought by Mr Willy James. His wife Evelyn became one of Edwardian society's best known hostesses. At this time, Edward, Prince of Wales, later King Edward VII was a frequent visitor to West Dean. Other Royal visitors included Queen Alexandra, the future King George V and Queen Mary, and King Alfonso XIII of Spain.

Mr Willy James died in 1912 and his estate was held in trust until his son, Edward (1907–1984) came of age. He was a poet, art collector and a major patron of the Surrealist movement. After the Second World War he spent much of his time abroad, living principally in Mexico. In 1964 he established the Edward James Foundation as a charitable educational trust. The house became a college, where traditional arts and crafts and the conservation and restoration of antiques are taught to a professional level.

The house is surrounded by 35 acres of gardens. There are water and wild gardens, through which the River Lavant flows, and a 300 foot long pergola designed by Harold Peto. The Edwardian walled kitchen garden is currently being refurbished.

Wild daffodils growing in St. Roche's Arboretum. The arboretum, which is located in the upper part of West Dean Park, is an area of sylvan peace and solitude and contains many exotic trees and shrubs from around the world.

The Weald and Downland Open Air Museum is a growing collection of rescued historic buildings from south east England, saved from destruction, dismantled and painstakingly re-erected on the museum site at Singleton.

The museum was established during the late 1960s by a small group of enthusiasts led by Dr Roy Armstrong. Its main task is to encourage the public to appreciate the rich heritage of vernacular buildings in the region.

The museum is continually developing and has nearly 40 buildings, which represent the traditional homes and workplaces of village and countryside. These include the re-created Bayleaf medieval farmstead, with its house and garden (*above*), and the market square with its Tudor market hall (*bottom right*). In addition, the museum aims to demonstrate some of the traditional rural crafts such as charcoal burning (*top right*).

A lively programme of special events with countryside themes, involving for example working heavy horses (*centre right*) takes place each year.

The open hall in Bayleaf, a timber-framed 15th century 'Wealden' farmhouse, has been furnished to show how it may have appeared in about 1540.

The yellow drawing room in Goodwood House contains a superb collection of Sevres porcelain. It is just one of the beautiful state apartments displaying the Goodwood collections of paintings by Stubbs, Canaletto and Van Dyck, furniture, tapestries and china.

Goodwood House has been the home of the Dukes of Richmond for 300 years. Built by the third Duke at
the end of the 18th century, it was designed by James Wyatt. The house and a number of buildings on the
Estate, built at this time, contain excellent examples of 'knapped' flintwork.

Goodwood House in winter.

The Festival of Speed.

(*Right*) Goodwood Golf Club and the 18th hole. The course was laid out by James Braid. The clubhouse was originally the kennels, designed by James Wyatt and built in 1787. The Hunt was moved from Charlton to Goodwood by the third Duke of Richmond.

Motor racing first came to Goodwood in 1936 when the Earl of March held a private hill climb through the Park for the Lancia Car Club. Five years earlier Freddie March had won the Brooklands Double 12. In 1948, as the ninth Duke of Richmond, he opened the Goodwood circuit. The circuit was built on the Westhampnett airfield, now Goodwood Aerodrome, a satellite airfield to RAF Tangmere during the Second World War. These early events inspired his grandson Charles March to revive motor sport in the Park and resulted in the Goodwood Festival of Speed.

The 1993 inaugural event was a huge success, reliving the great days of British Racing Green, featuring the world's greatest classic racing cars of the 1950s and 1960s.

Motor circuit with the racecourse on the Downs behind.

During the late 17th and first half of the 18th century, Charlton was the home of the country's premier foxhunt. The Duke of Monmouth hunted at Charlton and it is said that he wanted to establish his Court there should he become King. Another of Charles II's sons, the first Duke of Richmond, was also a keen huntsman. He purchased Goodwood a small hunting box near Charlton. Fox Hall, a hunting lodge, was built in the village by the second Duke in about 1730. The architect was either Lord Burlington or Roger Morris. It has been restored by the Landmark Trust and is let as holiday accommodation.

Goodwood panorama

Top class racing at Goodwood is enjoyed by racegoers on Trundle Hill. The racecourse is famous for its breath-taking views over the Sussex countryside, Chichester and the Solent.

King Edward VII's sentiment that racing at Goodwood is 'a garden party with racing tacked on' has been echoed down the years by race-goers and this unique atmosphere makes Goodwood the place to be and be seen. Due to Edward VII's influence panama hats gradually replaced the more formal racing attire of top hat and tails.

'Glorious Goodwood'.

A view from the Trundle, looking north towards the South Downs. 7,000 years ago this was a heavily wooded area. Since then, woodland clearance has created a very different landscape. The extensive areas of Charlton and Singleton forests seen on the skyline, were largely planted this century. The hill, centre right, with a mixture of shrubs and grassland on its slopes, is Levin Down, a nature reserve managed by Sussex Wildlife Trust.

132

The windmill, which is a prominent local landmark, stands on the top of Halnaker hill, commanding views of the coastal plain below. Part of the track leading to the mill is on the line of Stane Street, the Roman road that crosses the hill. The first reference to a mill was recorded in 1540. The present mill was built by the third Duke of Richmond for his tenants in about 1780. It fell into disrepair after a lightning strike in 1905. The mill was immortalised in a poem by Hilaire Belloc who lived at Slindon.

The sweep frames were restored in 1934 as a memorial to the wife of Sir William Bird, who lived nearby.

Boxgrove Priory viewed across a field of oilseed rape. This EC subsidised
crop has become a distinctive feature of the rural landscape in late spring.

The ruins of the priory guest house. The vaulted ground floor included the kitchen, with a great hall on the first floor and a guest room above.

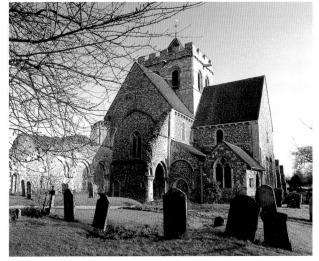

The Benedictine Priory of Boxgrove is one of the county's most important ecclesiastical buildings. The priory was founded in the early 12th century and was dissolved by King Henry VIII in 1537, leaving only the priory church for the villagers to worship in.

In 1622 the first reference to the game of cricket in Sussex was recorded, when six parishioners were prosecuted for playing the game in the churchyard on a Sunday.

Members of the 'Ermine Street Guard' participating in one of the special events held at the Roman palace every year.

The Roman palace at Fishbourne was discovered in 1960, when a workman cut into what proved to be the largest known Roman domestic building north of the Alps. It was one of the most important archaeological discoveries in Britain this century. Evidence suggests that the building may have been the palace of a local Celtic King, Cogidubnus.

Visitors to the site, which is owned by Sussex Past (Sussex Archaeological Society), can see the remains of the north wing enclosed within a modern cover building. Housed here is Britain's largest collection of 'in-situ' Roman mosaic floors, including the famous 'Cupid on a Dolphin'. There is an opportunity for visitors to make a mosaic of their own using stone *tesserae*.

The most important finds from the excavations are displayed in the museum along with explanatory pictures and models. Outside, it is possible to walk around the garden, which has been re-planted to its original Roman plan.

A school party admiring the mid-2nd century 'Cupid on a Dolphin' mosaic at the Roman palace.

Stansted Park, set in beautiful parkland, is one of the most elegant stately homes in the south of England. Home of Mary, the Countess and the late tenth Earl of Bessborough, it houses rare pieces of china and porcelain in the dining room and family portraits in the music room. The blue drawing room contains furniture brought over from France by the late Earl's mother.

'Below stairs' the old kitchen contains many original features and a superb array of copper utensils. Also on

show are the old staff quarters, housekeeper's room and servants' hall, which is used as an exhibition room.

A short stroll takes one to the ancient chapel with its unusual canopy supported on gilded wooden pillars and Regency gothic windows. Nearby is the arboretum with many fine deciduous and coniferous trees; there is also a walled garden which has been developed by Ivan Hicks into the Garden in Mind. The pavilion tea-room overlooks the cricket ground where matches are played on most Sundays in the summer.

Ivan Hicks, a garden designer and land artist, studied arboriculture and worked initially for Edward James at West Dean. He is particularly interested in historic and unusual gardens and in extending their usage or 'creating a laboratory of ideas'. His development of the old walled garden at Stansted into the Garden in Mind has attracted much interest. The garden is open to the public.

Kingley Vale is a National Nature Reserve managed by English Nature and is located four miles north west of Chichester. It is famous for its great yew forest which was probably first planted 500 years ago. A few of these ancient yews remain, but most of the trees are between 50 and 250 years old. At the turn of this century, the writer E.V. Lucas wrote 'Kingley Vale always grave and silent is transformed at dusk into a sinister and fantastic forest, the home for witchcraft and unquiet spirits'. Kingley Vale is also reputed to be the site of a battle,

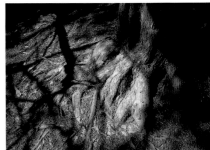

in which, according to the Anglo-Saxon Chronicle 'the men of Chichester slaughtered a Danish force' at the end of the 9th century. Whatever the truth behind this legend, there is evidence of a wide range of archaeological remains in the reserve; as well as a great number of different plants, birds, mammals and insects.

Racton Tower, a folly, was designed by Theodosius Keene in 1772 for Lord Halifax, owner of Stansted. The ruins of this well-known landmark still provoke a mysterious, ghostly atmosphere. It was a pleasure house, and local lore says that it was the haunt of smugglers, who used the top of the tower for signalling to boats bringing contraband into Chichester Harbour.

Stane Street runs close to Gumber Farm, a remote farmstead on the Downs near Slindon. One of the farm buildings has been converted by the National Trust into a bothy, where walkers and other users of the nearby South Downs Way can stay overnight.

Near Stoughton.

The control tower at Tangmere. Built in 1942, it is now only a sad reminder of the airfield's past importance.

RAF Tangmere played a major part in the Battle of Britain during the summer and autumn of 1940. Despite the station suffering severe damage in one raid by German dive bombers, the Tangmere Squadrons were instrumental in ensuring that the Luftwaffe failed in their efforts to overcome the RAF during this critical stage of the Second World War. Many famous pilots were stationed at Tangmere, including the legendary Douglas Bader who had been Squadron Leader of the Tangmere wing of the three Spitfire squadrons. He was at Tangmere from April 1941 until he was shot down over France in August of the same year.

The gravestones in St. Andrew's churchyard commemorate both British and German pilots who lost their lives during the war.

Tangmere Military Aviation Museum was founded by a few dedicated volunteers and opened in 1982. The museum's collections relate to military flying from its earliest days, with a particular emphasis on the history of Royal Air Force Tangmere and the air war over southern England from 1939 to 1945.

The museum is housed in buildings which date from the 1930s and were once used as radio repair workshops. A new hangar was built in 1992, and houses the actual Meteor and Hunter jet aircraft which broke the world air speed record, in 1964 and 1953 respectively, flying from Tangmere.

There is a large collection of photographs, paintings, documents, uniforms and medals which illustrate the story of this famous fighter airfield from its establishment in 1917 to its closure in 1970.

Between Goodwood and West Dean.

(*Left*) Seasons near Goodwood.

Since 1977 over 100,000 soldiers, police and civilians from all over the world have taken part in the Royal Military Police and City of Chichester International March. The last year of this popular annual event was 1993 when 5,500 people entered the march. Walkers are seen here coming down Chalkpit Lane from the Trundle, towards East Lavant. Chalkpit Lane once formed a part of the main coach road from Chichester to London.

Firemen battling with the rising water, in the Hornet, Chichester.

POSTSCRIPT

THE RIVER LAVANT
FLOODING

During January 1994 Chichester and the River Lavant
became the focus of media attention.
Exceptionally heavy autumn and winter rainfall caused the
tiny river to burst its banks, in contrast to recent years when
it failed to flow due to drought conditions.

Described by the National Rivers Authority as 'a one
in 200 year event', surrounding villages and the eastern side
of the city experienced some of the worst recorded flooding
in their history.

Constance Sutcliffe of Postcard Corner in the Almshouse Arcade, Chichester.

Children from the Welcome House day nursery wait to cross the Hornet, scene of the worst flooding in Chichester.

Another view of the Hornet, outside Cover's store.

Maureen Mason arranges the coal delivery, Merston. Whilst not on the course of the River Lavant, the hamlet of Merston was one of many places affected by the floods.

Lavant Green at the height of the flooding.

A thank you to the fire service.

ACKNOWLEDGEMENTS

We would like to thank the many people who have helped us in the compilation of this book by advising, lending photographs, providing information or contributing captions. We are most grateful to the following for their generous assistance; Miss L. Adams; Miss B. Andresen; Mr J. Buckland; the Headmaster of Chichester High School for Boys; Mr R. Carbines; the Administrator of the Clark Shoe Museum at Street; Mr. D. Coke; Mr J. Coppendale; Mr P. Couchman; Mr C. Fry; Miss S. Fullwood; Miss A. Griffiths; Mrs V. Griffiths; Mrs D.Harvey; Mr P. Hewitt; Mr I. Hicks; Mrs H. Jackson; Mr and Mrs C. Jones; the Rt. Reverend E. Knapp-Fisher, Custos to St. Mary's Hospital and Mrs G. Etherington, matron; Mr K. Leslie; Miss V. Lyon; Mr S. Kitchen; Mr J. McKerchar; Mr J. Magilton; Mr N. McGregor-Wood; Mr P. Moore; Dr. B. Pailthorpe; Mrs S. Papworth; Mr P. Parish; Mr R. Read; Mr D. Rudkin; Miss A. Sharp, St. Richards Hospital; Mr N. Smith; Mr and Mrs C. Upton; Mr R. Waite; Miss M. Ward; Mrs H. Way; Mr P. Weston; West Sussex County Council Library Service; West Sussex County Council Planning Department (Countryside Services); Mr R. Widdows; Mr N. Wild; Mr D. Wilkinson; Mr R. Williamson; Miss A. Wood; Miss L. Younger.

   In particular we would like to thank the Duke of Richmond for his vision and inspiration; Mrs J. Price and Mr S. Price for their help and for the loan of photographs from Bernard Price's collection used in the majority of the introduction; also Chichester District Museum; Dean and Chapter, Chichester Cathedral; the Manager of the Dolphin and Anchor Hotel and Mr I. Serraillier for the loan of photographs used in the remainder of the introduction; Mr K. Newbury, Editor of the *Chichester Observer* for permission to use the aerial photograph of Chichester on the front cover; Mr David Legg-Willis and Mrs Joy Whiting for their help, and Mrs Jane Pailthorpe for her infinite patience and much hard work typing the manuscript. Finally our grateful thanks to Geoff Farrell and Graham Russel of John Wiley & Sons Ltd for their support and assistance throughout the project.

PHOTOGRAPHIC CREDITS

All photographs by Iain McGowan F.R.P.S. except for the following:

Louise Adams — pages 51, 52, 61, 120 (*centre*).

Martyn Elford, Autosport — page 126 (*top right*).

Paul Biddle — page 120 (*top right*).

Chichester Observer — jacket and page 42.

The Trustees of the Goodwood Collections — page 124.

Gary Hawkins — page 127 (*top right*).

Michael Moore — page 66 (*right*).

Richard Pailthorpe — pages 13, 22 (*right*), 29 (*left*), 34 (*right*), 35 (*right*), 38 (*right*), 44 (*bottom right*), 45 (*left*), 56 (*right*), 72 (*left*), 108 (*centre left*), 110 (*right*), 122, 126 (*top left and bottom*), 134.

Pallant House — page 136 (*both*).

St. Richard's Hospital — page 58 (*bottom*).

David Rudkin — page 136 (*left*).

Stansted Park — page 138 (*bottom right*).

John Timbers — page 55 (*left*).

Harold Turner — page 94 (*right*).

Weald and Downland Open Air Museum — page 123.

Joy Whiting — pages 67 (*right*), 120 (*bottom right*).

FURTHER READING

There are numerous books, booklets, papers and guides about Chichester and the surrounding area. It is impossible to list all of them but the following have been most useful and it is recommended that anyone interested in seeking more detailed information should refer to them.

Armstrong, J.R., *A History of Sussex*, Phillimore, 1974

Bessborough, Earl of, *Enchanted Forest*, Weidenfeld and Nicholson, 1984

Bishop, J.H., *A Sussex Pot-Pourri*, 1986

Brandon, P., *The Sussex Landscape*, Hodder & Stoughton, 1974

Bromley-Martin, A., *Around Chichester*, 1991

Bromley-Martin, A., *Chichester Harbour, Past and Present*, Hughenden Publications, 1991

Brunnarius, M., *Windmills of Sussex*, Phillimore, 1979

Chichester College of Arts, Science and Technology Prospectus

Chichester District Guidebooks

Chichester High School for Boys Prospectus

Chichester Observer Series

Clifton-Taylor, A., *Chichester*, EDC, 1984

Coke D., *Pallant House — Its Architecture, History and Owners*, 1993

Dallaway, J., *History of West Sussex*, Vols. 1 and 2, 1815

Down, A., *Roman Chichester*, Phillimore, 1988

Evershed-Martin, L., *The Impossible Theatre*, Phillimore, 1988

Fishbourne Roman Palace Guidebook

Godfrey, J., Leslie, K., Zeuner, D., *Very Special County. West Sussex County Council, The First 100 Years*, West Sussex County Council, 1988

Guidebooks to Boxgrove Priory, Apuldram, Eartham, Selsey and Upwaltham churches

Harmer, R., *Chichester in Old Photographs*, Alan Sutton, 1990

Heneghen, F.D., 'The Chichester Canal', *Chichester Papers*, 1958

Holtby, R.I., *Chichester Cathedral Guidebook*, Pitkin Pictorials Ltd, 1991

Hudson, W.H., *Nature in Downland*, J.M. Dent, 1923

Hunn, D., *Goodwood*, Davis-Poynter, 1975

Keating, L. *The Book of Chichester*, Barracuda Books, 1979

Lucas, E.V., *Highways and Byways in Sussex*, Macmillan, 1904

McCann, A., *A Short History of the City of Chichester and its Cathedral*, WSRO, 1985

McCann, T.J., *Restricted Grandeur Chichester*, 1586–1948, WSRO, 1974

Mee, A., *Sussex*, Hodder & Stoughton, 1937

Mee, F., *A History of Selsey*, Phillimore, 1988

Morgan, R., *Chichester — A Documentary History*, Phillimore, 1992

Morris, J., *The History of the Selsey Lifeboats*, R.N.L.I., 1986

Munby, J., *St. Mary's Hospital Guide*, 1987

Nairn and Pevsner, *The buildings of England, Sussex*, Penguin, 1965

Newbury, K., *The River Lavant*, Phillimore, 1987

Ogley, Currie and Davison, *The Sussex Weather Book*, Froglets Publications, 1991

Ollernshaw, P., *The History of the Prebendal School*, Phillimore, 1984

Pailthorpe, R., and Serraillier, I., *Goodwood Country in Old Photographs*, Alan Sutton, 1987

Parish, W.D., *A Dictionary of the Sussex Dialect*, republished, Gardner's Bexhill, 1957

Price, B., *Sussex, People, Places and Things*, Phillimore, 1975

Price. B., *Bygone Chichester*, Phillimore, 1975

Price, B., *The Valiant Years*, Phillimore, 1978

Price, B., *Changing Chichester*, Phillimore, 1982

Sarginson, P.(ed.), *The Edward James Foundation*, 1992

Serraillier, I., *All Change at Singleton*, Phillimore, 1979

Smith, W.J., *Sussex Smugglers*, Brighton

Stansted Park Guidebook

Tangmere Military Aviation Museum Guidebook

Steer, F.W., 'The Dolphin and Anchor Hotel', *Chichester Papers*, No. 23, 1960

Steer, F.W., 'The Memoirs of James Spershott', *Chichester Papers*, No. 30, 1962

Steer, F.W., 'The Grange, Tower Street', *Chichester Papers*, No. 39, 1963

The Chichester Canal Guide, Chichester Canal Society

The Chichester Harbour Landscape, Countryside Commission

The Victoria County History of Sussex, Vols. 3 and 4

Weald and Downland Open Air Museum Guidebook

West Sussex Institute of Higher Education Prospectus

Williamson, R., *The Great Yew Forest*, Macmillan, 1978

Willis, T.G., *Records of Chichester*, 1928

Wilson, A.E., 'Archaeology of the City Walls', *Chichester Papers*, No. 6, 1957

PLACES OF INTEREST TO VISIT

The following are members of the Chichester Visitors Group, which is a consortium of the main visitor attractions in and around Chichester. The C.V.G. as it is often called has been described as 'a unique Collection of Rareties'.

Chichester Cathedral, Tel : (0243) 782595
Chichester Festival Theatre, Tel : (0243) 784437
Chichester District Museum, Tel : (0243) 784683
Pallant House, Tel : (0243) 774557
Chichester Festivities, Tel : (0243) 785718
Mechanical Music and Doll Collection, Tel : (0243) 785421
Stansted Park, Tel : (0705) 412265
Fishbourne Roman Palace, Tel : (0243) 785859
Goodwood House, Tel : (0243) 774107
Weald and Downland Open Air Museum, Tel : (0243) 811348
West Dean College and Gardens, Tel : (0243) 811301
Tangmere Military Aviation Museum, Tel : (0243) 775223
Chichester Harbour Conservancy, Tel : (0243) 512301
Chichester Harbour Water Tours, Tel : (0243) 786418

For further information telephone the above numbers, or contact Chichester Tourist Information Office, Tel : (0243) 775888, who also have details of other places of interest to visit.